Rainer Maria Rilke

Rainer Maria Rilke

LETTERS TO A YOUNG POET
Translated by **K. W. Maurer**

POEMS
Translated by **Jessie Lemont**

BLACK EAGLE BOOKS
Dublin, USA | Bhubaneswar, India

Black Eagle Books
   USA address:
7464 Wisdom Lane
Dublin, OH 43016

India address:
E/312, Trident Galaxy, Kalinga Nagar,
Bhubaneswar-751003, Odisha, India

E-mail: info@blackeaglebooks.org
Website: www.blackeaglebooks.org

First International Edition Published by
Black Eagle Books, 2023

LETTERS TO A YOUNG POET
by Rainer Maria Rilke
Translated by **K. W. Maurer**

POEMS
by Rainer Maria Rilke
Translated by **Jessie Lemont**

Copyright © BEB

Cover & Interior Design: Ezy's Publication

ISBN- 978-1-64560-430-3 (Paperback)

Printed in the United States of America

LETTERS TO A YOUNG POET
Translated by K. W. Maurer

Introduction

IT was in the late autumn of 1902 — I was sitting under some century-old chestnut trees in the park of the Military Academy in Wiener-Neustadt reading a book. I was so engrossed in my reading that I hardly noticed that the only one of our masters who was not an officer, the learned kindly chaplain of the Academy, Horaček, had joined me. He took the volume out of my hand, considered the binding, and shook his head. "Rainer Maria Rilke's Poems"? he asked thoughtfully. Then he turned over the leaves here and there, scanned a few verses, looked thoughtfully into the distance, and finally nodded. "So young René Rilke has become a poet."

And I heard about the small, pale boy, whom his parents had sent more than fifteen years before to the military Lower Military School in Sankt-Pölten, intending that he should afterwards become an officer. At that time Horaček had been working there as chaplain of the establishment, and he still remembered the boy of those days perfectly. He painted him as a quiet, earnest, extremely clever young fellow, who liked keeping to himself, put up patiently with the discipline of the boarding school and after his fourth year passed on with the others to the Military College, which was in Mährisch-Weisskirchen. Then his constitution showed itself definitely not to be strong enough, so that his parents removed him from the school and let him continue his studies at home in Prague. Horaček could tell me nothing more of the course which his outward life had taken since then.

After all that, I think it is easy to understand that I decided at that very moment to send my efforts in poetry to Rainer Maria Rilke and to ask him for his verdict. I was not yet twenty years old and I was just on the threshold of a career which I felt to be directly opposed to my inclinations. From the author of "Mir zur Feier," if from anyone at all, I hoped for sympathetic understanding. And though I had not so intended, I came to write a letter with my verses, in which I opened my heart without reticence, as never before or since to another human being.

Many weeks passed before an answer came. The blue, sealed letter had a Paris post-mark and felt heavy in my hands; the envelope bore the same beautiful, clear handwriting as that in which the whole text from the first lines to the last had been written. That was the beginning of my regular correspondence with Rainer Marie Rilke, which continued till 1908 and then gradually came to an end, because my life drove me into the very paths from which the poet's warm, affectionate and moving concern had wished to preserve me.

But that is of no importance. Alone important are the ten letters which follow, important for the knowledge of the world, in which Rainer Maria Rilke lived and created, and to many human beings of to-day and to-morrow, who are growing and coming into being. When a great and exceptional man speaks, the insignificant must be silent.

FRANZ XAVER KAPPUS.
Berlin, June 1929

THE LETTERS

Letter One

Dear Sir,

Your letter only reached me a few days ago. I should like to thank you for its great and touching confidence. I can do little more. I cannot go into the nature of your verses, for any intention to criticise is too foreign to me. Nothing can touch a work of art so little as words of criticism: they always result in more or less happy misunderstandings. Things are not all so easy to grasp and to express as most people would have us believe; most events are inexpressible, and take place in a sphere that no word has ever entered. Most inexpressible of all are works of art, existences full of secrets whose life continues alongside ours, whilst ours is transitory.

Only when I have first drawn your attention to that fact, can I then tell you that your verses have no special nature of their own, yet show a quiet and concealed inclination towards the personal. I have that feeling most strongly in the last poem, "My Soul." There it is something of your own that is trying to find expression in words and melody. And in the beautiful poem, "To Leopardi," I think a kind of relationship with this great solitary man may be growing up.

Yet your poems, even the last one and the one to Leopardi, are as yet nothing in themselves, nothing independent. Your kind letter which accompanied them does not fail to explain to me many deficiencies which I felt in reading your verses without being able to put a name to them.

You ask me if your verses are good. You ask me. You have asked others before me. You send them to journals. You compare them with other poems and you worry if certain editors refuse your efforts. Now, as you have given me permission to advise you, I beg you to give up all that. You are directing your thoughts outwards, and that above all is what you should not do at present. No one can advise and help you, no one. There is only one way. Withdraw into yourself. Explore the reason that bids you write, find out if it has spread out its roots in the very depths of your heart; confess to yourself whether you would have to die, if writing should be denied to you. Above all, ask yourself in the stillest hour of the night, "Must I write?" Dig deep into yourself for an answer. And if this answer should be in the affirmative, if you can meet this solemn question with a simple strong "I must," then build up your life according to this necessity. Your life right down to its most indifferent and unimportant hour must be a token and a witness to this compulsion. Then approach nature. Try to express what you see and experience and love and lose as if you were the first man alive. Do not write love-poems. Avoid those forms which are too trite and commonplace: they are the hardest, for a great and mature power is needed to give of one's own where good and often brilliant traditions throng upon one. Therefore betake yourself from the usual themes to those which your everyday life offers you. Paint your sadnesses and your desires, your passing thoughts and your belief in some kind of beauty—paint all that with quiet and modest inward sincerity; and to express yourself use the things that surround you, the pictures of your dreams and the objects of your recollections. When your daily life seems barren, do not blame it; blame yourself rather and tell yourself that you are not poet enough to call forth its riches; for the creative worker knows no barrenness and no poor indifferent place. And even if you were in a prison, whose walls prevented all the bustle of the world from reaching your senses, even then would you not still have your childhood, that precious, kingly wealth, that treasure-house of memories? Turn your attention towards it. Try to recall the forgotten sensations of that distant past; your personality will strengthen itself, your loneliness will extend itself and become a dusky dwelling and the noise of others will pass by it far away. And when from this turning inwards, from this retreat into your own world verses come into being, then you will not think of asking anyone, whether they are good verses. Nor will you try to get journals interested in these works, for you will see in them your own loved and natural possession, a part and an expression of your life. A work of art is good, when it is born of necessity. In this question of its origin lies the criterion according to which it may be judged. There is no other. Therefore, dear Sir, I would give you no advice but this—to retire into yourself and sound the depths in which your life has its source; at its source you will find the answer to the question whether you must create. Accept it just as it is, without trying to interpret it. Perhaps it will be shown that you are called to be an artist. Then take your destiny upon your shoulders and bear it with its burden and its greatness without ever asking for the reward which might come from without. For the creator must be a world in himself and must find everything in himself and in nature, to whom he has attached himself.

But perhaps even after this retreat into yourself and into your solitude you will have to renounce the idea of becoming a poet. As I said, the feeling that one could live without writing is enough to prove that one should not write at all. But even so, this contemplation which I beg you to make will not have been in vain. In any case your life will thereafter find out its own course, and I hope for you more sincerely than I can say that it may be good, rich and wide.

What else am I to say to you? I think I have given every point the right emphasis; finally I should like to give you just this one other piece of advice, to follow quietly and earnestly the course of your development. You cannot disturb it more drastically than if you direct your thoughts outwards and expect from without the answer to questions which probably only your innermost feeling in the quietest hour of your life can answer.

It was a joy to me to find the name of Professor Horaček in your letter. For that lovable scholar I have cherished a respect and a gratitude which lasts through the passing years. Will you please tell him of my feeling for him. It is very kind of him to remember me still and I know how to value it.

At the same time I give you back again the verses which you were kind enough to entrust to me, and again I thank you for your great and affectionate confidence. By this sincere answer, which I have given to the best of my ability, I have tried to make myself a little worthier of it than, as a stranger, I really am.

With all respect and sympathy,

Rainer Maria Rilke

Letter Two

Viareggio, near Pisa, Italy,

5th April, 1903.

You must forgive me, my dear Sir, that it is only to-day that I remember with gratitude your letter of the 24th February. I was unwell the whole time, not exactly ill, but suffering from a kind of influenza-weakness, which rendered me incapable of doing anything. Finally, as my health would not change at all, I came to this salutary southern sea, which helped me once before, but I am not yet returned to health and I find writing difficult, so you must take these few lines for more.

Naturally you must know that every letter of yours will always delight me; you must only be indulgent about the answer, which will probably often leave you empty-handed; for at bottom, and just in the profoundest and most important matters, we are inexpressibly alone, and for one man to be able to advise or even help another, many things must happen, many things must succeed, a whole constellation of circumstances must converge, for it once to turn out happily.

I should only like to say two things to you to-day. First:

Do not allow yourself to be mastered by irony, especially in uncreative moments. In creative moments try to make use of it, but only as one more means to grasp hold of life. If its use is pure, it is itself pure also, and one must not be ashamed of it. If you feel that you are too familiar with it, if you are afraid of your growing familiarity with it, then turn to great and solemn objects, before which it becomes small and helpless. Seek the depth of things, for irony never penetrates there—and when you go thus to the edge of what is great, find out at the same time whether this form of comprehension arises from a necessity of your being. Under the influence of solemn events, it will either fall away from you, if it is a thing of chance, or, if it really belongs to you and is innate in you, it will grow stronger and become a serious tool and take its place among the means by which you will have to build up your art.

And the second thing I should like to tell you to-day is this:

Of all my books there are only a few which are indispensable to me, and two of them are actually always among my belongings, wherever I am. I have them with me here, too, the Bible and the books of the great Danish poet, Jens Peter Jacobsen. I wonder whether you know his works. You can easily get hold of them, for some of them have appeared in a very good translation in "Reclams Universal Bibliothek." Get hold of the little volume, "Six Stories," by J. P. Jacobsen and of his novel, "Niels Lyhne," and in the first little volume begin the first story which is called "Mogens." A world will come over you, a happiness, a wealth, a world of inconceivable greatness. Live for awhile in these books, learn from them what seems to you worth learning, but above all, love them. This love will be repaid a thousandfold, and, whatever may become of your life will, I am convinced of it, run through the fabric of your being as one of the most important among all the threads of your experiences, disappointments and joys.

If I am to speak of the sources from which I learnt anything concerning the nature of creative work, concerning its depths and its everlastingness, there are only two names which I can mention: that of Jacobsen, that great, great poet, and that of Auguste Rodin, the sculptor, who has not his equal among all the artists who are living to-day.

And may happy fulfilment in everything attend upon the paths of your life.

Yours,

Rainer Maria Rilke

Letter Three

Your Easter letter, my dear Sir, has caused me much joy; for it spoke much good of you, and the manner in which you spoke of Jacobsen's great and lovely art, showed me that I have not been wrong in leading your life and its many questions to this well of plenteousness.

Now "Niels Lyhne" will disclose itself to you, a book of the things of grandeur and of depth. The more one reads it, the more it seems to contain everything from the most delicate fragrances of life to the full and grand flavours of its hardest fruits. In it there is nothing that has not been understood, grasped, experienced and recognised in the vibrating echoes of the memory; no experience has been too small, the slightest occurrence unfolds itself like a destiny. Destiny itself is like a wonderful broad web in which each thread is pulled by an infinitely tender hand and is laid by the side of another and held up and borne along by hundreds of others. You will experience the happiness of reading this book for the first time, and will pass through countless surprises, as in a new dream. But I can tell you that later, too, one always remains the same wonderer when going through these books, and that they lose nothing of the wonderful force and relinquish nothing of the fabulousness with which they overwhelm the reader the first time.

The enjoyment of them and the gratitude only grows ever greater, and one's way of looking at things becomes somehow better and simpler, one's belief in life deeper and one's life itself more blessed and more significant.

Later you must read the wonderful book of the fate and the yearning of "Marie Grubbe," and Jacobsen's letters and journal and fragments, and finally his verses, which though only moderately translated live in unending music. [For that purpose I should advise you to buy at your convenience the beautiful edition of Jacobsen's collected works, which contains all that. It appeared in Leipzig in three volumes in a good translation at Eugen Diederichs and, I think, only costs 5 or 6 marks a volume.]

In your opinion about "Here should roses stand . . ." —that work so incomparable in its delicacy and form—you are of course quite, quite indisputably in the right against the man who wrote the introduction. And I may as well make this request of you here: read as few works of aesthetic criticism as possible—there are in them either partisan opinions which have become petrified and meaningless in their lifeless obduracy, or else a clever play of words, with which to-day one view finds favour and tomorrow the opposite. Works of art are of an infinite loneliness and nothing can reach them so little as criticism. Only love can grasp them and keep hold of them and be just to them. Always trust yourself and your own feelings as opposed to any such analysis, review or introduction; if you should be wrong, then the natural growth of your inner life will lead you slowly and in time to new realisations. Allow your judgments their own quiet, undisturbed development, which like all progress must come from deep within you and cannot be forced or hastened by anything. The whole thing is to carry the full time and then give birth; to let every impression and every germ of a feeling consummate itself entirely within itself, in that which is dark, inexpressible, unconscious and unattainable by your own intelligence, and to await the hour of the delivery of a new clearness of vision. That alone is to live an artistic life, in understanding, as in creating.

In that there is no measuring with time; no year is of any value and ten years are as nothing. To be an artist is this: not to count or to reckon: to ripen like a tree which does not force its sap, but in the storms of spring stands confident without being afraid that afterwards no summer may come. The summer comes all right. But it only comes to the patient, to those who are there as carefree and quiet and immense, as if eternity lay before them. Daily I learn, learn it through my sufferings [to which I am grateful] that patience is everything.

Richard Dehmel: His books—and I may say the same thing of the man, whom I know slightly—have the following effect upon me, that, when I have found one of his beautiful pages, I am always afraid of the next, which may upset everything again and pervert the lovable into the unworthy. You characterised him very well with the expression: "sensual life and sensual poetry"—and it is undoubtedly a fact that artistic experience has such an inconceivably close connection with sexual experience, with its pain and its desire, that the two phenomena are actually nothing but two different forms of one and the same yearning and bliss. And if instead of sensuality one could say sex—sex in its great, wide and pure sense, free from the suspicion cast upon it by errors of the Church—then his art would be very great and infinitely important. His poetical power is great and strong as a primeval impulse. It has its own independent rhythms, and breaks forth from him like a stream from the mountains.

But I think that this power is not always quite sincere and without pose [this is actually one of the severest tests for the creator: he must always remain unconscious, without an idea of his greatest qualities, if he does not want to rob them of their naiveté and their virginity!] And then, when rushing through his being it comes to the sexual, it finds there a man who is not so utterly pure as it needed him to be. Here is a sexual world that is not quite ripe and pure, one that is not human enough but only male, one that is sensuality, intoxication and restlessness, burdened with the old prejudices and insolence with which man has deformed and burdened love. Because he only loves as a man and not as a human being, therefore there is in his sexual sensibility a narrowness, an ostensible wildness and hate, something transient and mortal, which detracts from his art and renders it ambiguous and undecided. It is not without defect, it is marked by time and by passion and little of it will last and endure. [But most art is like that!] But in spite of that, one can get deep enjoyment, from what is great in it, and must only take care not to lose oneself in it and not to become an adherent of Dehmel's world, which is so infinitely frightened, full of adultery and confusion, and far removed from those our actual destinies, which cause more suffering than these transient troubles, but at the same time give more opportunity for greatness and more courage for eternity.

Lastly as far as concerns my books, I should have

liked best of all to send you all those that could give you any pleasure, but I am very poor, and, once they have been published, my books no longer belong to me. I cannot myself buy them, and, as I should so often like, give them to those who would handle them with affection.

So I have written down for you on a scrap of paper the titles and publishers of my latest books—of the most recent only—in all I have published about 12 or 15—and I must leave it to you, dear Sir, to order some of them for yourself at your own convenience.

I like to know that my books are in your hands.

Farewell,

Yours,

Rainer Maria Rilke

Letter Four

Worpswede, near Bremen,

16th July, 1903.

I left Paris about ten days ago, thoroughly unwell and tired, and travelled to a great northerly plain, whose expanse, quiet and sky are to return me to health again. But I met with a long period of rain, which is trying to-day for the first time to clear up over the restlessly storm-driven land. I make use of this first moment of brightness to greet you, dear Sir.

My very dear Herr Kappus, I have left a letter of yours long unanswered—not that I had forgotten it; on the contrary it was of the kind which one reads again, when one finds it among one's letters, and in it I seemed to get to know you, as it were, most intimately. It was the letter of the 2nd May and I am sure that you remember it. When I read it as now in the great stillness of these distant parts, then your beautiful concern for life moves me, moves me even more than it moved me in Paris, where everything strikes the ear differently and fades away before the excessive, the earth-shaking noise. Here, where a mighty land is about me, here I feel that no human being can answer for you those questions and feelings which have a life of their own in the depth of your heart, for even the best use words wrongly when they want to give them the most delicate and almost inexpressible meaning. But, for all that, I think that you cannot remain without a solution, if you attach yourself to objects like those with which my eyes are now regaling themselves. If you attach yourself to Nature, to the simple and small in her, which hardly anyone sees, but which can so unexpectedly turn into the great and the immeasurable, if you have this love for what is slight and try quite simply as a servant to win the confidence of what appears to you poor, then everything will become easier for you, more uniform and somehow more reconciling, not perhaps in the understanding, which holds back in amazement, but in your innermost consciousness, watchfulness and knowledge. You are so young, all beginning is so far in front of you, and I should like to beg you earnestly to have patience with all unsolved problems in your heart and to try to love the questions themselves like locked rooms, or books that are written in a foreign tongue. Do not search now for the answers, which cannot be given you, because you could not live them. That is the point, to live everything. Now you must live your problems. And perhaps gradually, without noticing it, you will live your way into the answer some distant day. Perhaps you actually have in you the possibility of moulding and shaping, as a particularly blessed and pure form of life; train yourself in it—but take what comes in complete trust, and, as long as it comes from your own will, from some need or other of your inner self, then take it for itself and hate nothing. Sex is difficult, yes, it is difficult. But the things with which we have been charged are difficult, almost everything serious is difficult, and everything is serious. If only you realise that and manage out of yourself, out of your predisposition and nature, out of your experience and your childhood and your own resources, to win a relation to sex entirely your own and free from the influence of convention or custom, then you must no longer fear to lose yourself and to become unworthy of your best possession.

Bodily pleasure is an experience of the senses, exactly like pure seeing or the pure feeling with which a lovely fruit fills the tongue; it is a great and infinite experience which is given to us, a knowledge of the world, the fulfilment and glory of all knowledge. And it is not our receiving it that is bad; what is bad is that nearly everybody misuses and squanders this experience and, instead of storing it up for supreme moments, uses it as an allurement and a distraction at the tired moments of his life. Eating, too, has been turned by mankind into something else; want on the one hand and excess on the other have rendered turbid the clearness of this need, and all the deep and simple necessities in which life renews itself have in like manner become turbid. But the individual man can make them clear for himself and live clearly [or if not the individual who is too dependent, at any rate the solitary man]. He can remember that all beauty in animals and plants is a quiet and lasting form of love and longing, and he can see the animal, as he sees the plant, patiently and willingly synthesising and increasing itself and growing net out of physical desire or physical pain, but bending to necessities which are greater than desire and pain and mightier than will and resistance. Oh, that mankind would receive more humbly this secret, of which the earth right down to its smallest things is full, and would bear it and endure it more seriously, and would feel how terribly difficult it is, instead of taking it so lightly! If he would only show respect towards his fruitfulness, which is only one and the same whether its manifestation be spiritual or physical; for spiritual creation, too, springs originally from the physical, is of one essence with it, and is simply like a more delicate, more enraptured, and more eternal, repetition of bodily pleasure. "The thought of being a creative worker, of begetting, of shaping" is nothing without its great and lasting confirmation and realisation in the world, nothing without the thousand-fold assent of animals and things—and only for this reason is its enjoyment so indescribably lovely and rich, that it is full of inherited recollections of the begetting and bearing of millions. In one thought of a creative worker a thousand forgotten nights of love come to life again and fill it with loftiness and sublimity. And those, who come together in the night and are twined in quivering pleasure, are performing a serious work and are heaping up sweetness, depth and force for the song of some coming poet, who will arise to express inexpressible ecstasies. Therewith they call to the future, and if ever they err and embrace blindly, the future comes all the same, a new man arises, and on the ground of Chance, which here appears ratified, there awakes the law by which the more resistant and more powerful seed makes its way to the open cell which advances towards it. Do not be led astray by the surface of things; in the depths everything becomes law. And those who live this secret falsely and badly—and they are very many—lose it only for themselves and still hand it on unconsciously like a closed letter. Do not be led astray by multiplicity of names and the complicatedness of occasions. Perhaps there exists over everything a mighty motherhood in the form of universal yearning. The beauty of the young virgin woman, a being who, as you so beautifully put it, has not yet performed her task, is motherhood, which has a presentiment of itself and prepares itself, is anxious and yearns. The mother's beauty is serving motherhood, and in the old woman it is a mighty recollection. And I think that there is motherhood in man too, bodily and spiritual motherhood; his begetting is a kind of bearing, too, and bearing it is, when he creates out of his innermost abundance. Perhaps the sexes are more related to each other than is supposed, and the great renovation of the world will perhaps consist in this, that men and women, freed from all confused feelings and aversion, will seek each other out not as contrasts but as brothers and sisters and as neighbours, and will work together as human beings to bear seriously and patiently in common this heavy burden of sex which has been laid upon them.

But everything that will perhaps some time be possible for many, the solitary man can already prepare and build up with his hands, which err less than others. Therefore, dear Sir, love your solitude, and bear the pain which it causes you with euphonious lament. For you say that those who are near to you are far away, and that shows that your outlook is beginning to be wide. And if your foreground is far from you, then your horizon is already beneath the stars and very great. Rejoice in your growth, into which you can take no one with you, and be good to those who remain behind. Be assured and peaceful in their presence, do not torture them with your doubts and do not frighten them with your confidence or your joy, which they could not comprehend. Seek some kind of simple, true communion with them, which need not change as you yourself become ever different. Love in them life in a form unknown to you, and be indulgent towards those who, as they grow old, fear that solitude in which you have confidence. Avoid adding new material to that strained drama which- is ever played between parents and children. It uses up much of the children's strength and consumes the love of the parents, which is always active and warm, even if it does not understand. Do not ask them for any advice and reckon on no understanding from them, but believe in a love which is stored up for you as a heritage, and have confidence that in this love there is a force and a blessedness, which you need never leave behind even in your furthest journeys.

It is a good thing that you are now entering upon a career which makes you independent and sets you entirely on your own feet in every sense. Wait patiently to see whether your innermost life feels itself limited by the nature of this career. I consider that it is very difficult and makes very many claims upon one, for it is burdened with great conventions and leaves hardly any room for a personal interpretation of its duties. But your loneliness will be a support and a home to you in the midst of unsympathetic surroundings, and out of it you will find all the ways of your life. All my good wishes are ready to accompany you, and my confidence is with you.

Yours,

Rainer Maria Rilke.

Letter Five

Rome, 29th
October, 1903

My dear Sir,

I received your letter of the 29th August at Florence, and it is only after two months that I now speak to you about it. Please forgive me this tardiness, but I do not like writing letters on a journey, because for letter-writing I need something more than the necessary tools — a little quiet and solitude and a not too unfriendly hour.

We reached Rome about six weeks ago, at a time when it was still the empty, hot Rome notorious for its fever, and this circumstance, together with other practical difficulties in our arrangements, helped to bring it about that our restlessness would have no end and that the foreign country weighed upon us with the burden of homelessness. I must add, that, if one does not know it, Rome has an oppressive and saddening effect during the first days because of the lifeless and unhealthy atmosphere of museums which it exhales, because of the numberless monuments of the past, which have been hauled out and laboriously restored, and from which a tiny present draws nourishment, and because of the dreadful over-estimation of these deformed and ruined objects, which is supported by philologists and copied by the conventional Italian tourists; though at bottom they are nothing more than the chance remains of another epoch and of a life which is not, and should not be, ours. Finally, after weeks of daily self-defence, though still a little bewildered, one comes to oneself again and one says, "No, there is no more beauty here than elsewhere, and all these objects, which generation after generation has continued to admire and which the hands of jobbers have repaired and restored, mean nothing, are nothing, and have no heart and no value"; but there is plenty of beauty here, because there is plenty of beauty everywhere. Waters infinitely full of life flow over the old aqueducts into the great town. They dance in its many squares over white stone bores and spread themselves out in broad roomy basins. They murmur by day and lift up their murmuring by night, which is vast here and starry and soft with breezes. And there are gardens here, unforgettable avenues and staircases, staircases thought out by Michelangelo, staircases which are built in the likeness of downward-gliding waters—the steps in their broad descent-giving birth one to the other like waves. By such impressions does one pull oneself together and win oneself back from all the claims of the many things which talk and chatter here—and how talkative they are!—and one learns slowly to recognise the few things in which there dwells eternity, which one can love, and solitude, in which one can quietly share.

I am still living in the town on the Capitol, not far from the most beautiful image of a horseman which has remained preserved for us from Roman art—that of Marcus Aurelius. But in a few weeks I shall move into a quiet and simple room, an old gallery lying deep in the heart of a large park, hidden from the town with its noise and incidents. I shall live there the whole winter and rejoice in the great quietness, from which I am hoping for the gift of good and profitable hours.

From there, where I shall be more at home, I will write you a longer letter, in which I will also talk about your writing. To-day I must only tell you what I have perhaps been wrong in not telling you earlier, that the book whose despatch you announced in your letter, and which should contain some of your work, has not arrived here. Did it go back to you from Worpswede? Because one is not permitted to forward parcels to foreign countries. That is the best thing that can have happened to it, and I would be glad to hear it confirmed. I hope it is not a question of loss, which is unfortunately far from being an exceptional occurrence with the Italian postal system.

I should have been glad to receive this book, as indeed anything which gives an indication of yourself, and if you entrust to me any verses that have come into being in the meantime, I will read them as well and truly from my heart as I can.

With good wishes and greetings,

Yours,

Rainer Maria Rilke.

Letter Six

My dear Herr Kappus,

You shall not be without a greeting from me at Christmastime, when in the midst of this festivity your loneliness weighs more heavily upon you than usually. But when you notice that it is great, rejoice in it; for you must ask yourself what that loneliness would be, that had not greatness; there is only one kind of loneliness. It is great and not easy to bear, and there comes to nearly everyone the hours, when he would gladly exchange it for any intercourse however common-place and cheap, for the semblance of a slight understanding with the next best, with the most unworthy. . . . But perhaps those are just the hours when the loneliness grows; for its growing is as painful as the growing of boys and as sad as the beginning of spring. But that should not confuse you. It is still only loneliness that is necessary—great inner loneliness. To retreat into oneself and meet nobody for hours on end—that is what one must be able to attain. To be alone, as one was alone as a child, when the grown-ups walked about involved in things which seemed great and important, because big people looked so busy and because one could comprehend nothing of their doings. And when one day one realises that their affairs are paltry, their professions benumbed and no longer connected with life, why not still like a child look upon them as something strange from without the depth of one's own world, regarding them from the immunity of one's own loneliness, which is itself work, position and profession? Why desire to exchange a child's wise incomprehension for self-defence and disdain? Incomprehension is loneliness, but self-defence and disdain are participation in that from which one is trying to separate oneself by these means.

Consider the world which you carry within you, and call this consideration what you like; let it be recollections of your own childhood or yearning for your own future—only be attentive to that which rises up within you, and place it above everything that you see around you. The events of your innermost self are worthy of your whole love. You must somehow work at them and not lose too much time or too much spirit in elucidating your position with regard to mankind. Who, pray, says that you have any such position? I know that your profession is hard and full of opposition to yourself; I foresaw your complaint and knew that it would come. Now that it has come I cannot soothe it. I can only advise you to consider whether all professions are not like that, full of claims, full of enmity for the individual, and at the same time fully imbued with the hate of those who submit dumbly and surlily to monotonous duty. The position in which you must now live is no more heavily burdened with conventions, prejudices and errors than other positions, and if there are some which carry with them a greater outward freedom, there is none that in itself is wide and spacious and connected with the great things of which real life consists. Only the individual, who is lonely, is like a thing placed under obscure laws, and whether a man goes out into the morning as it rises, or looks out into the eventful evening, and feels what is happening there, all position falls away from him as from a dead man, although he is standing in the middle of real life. What you are experiencing now as an officer, you would have felt in like manner in any of the existing professions, and even if apart from any position, you had sought easy and independent contact with society alone, this feeling of constraint would still not have been spared you. Everywhere it is the same, but that is no reason for anxiety or sadness. If there is no intercourse between you and mankind, try to get nearer to "things." They will not desert you; there are still the nights and the winds which blow through the trees and over many lands; with "things" and with animals, everything is still full of happenings in which you can take part; and children are still the same as you were as a child, so sad and so happy—and when you think of your childhood, then you live again among them, among the lonely children, and the grown-ups are nothing and their dignity has no value.

And if it makes you anxious and torments you to think of childhood and the simplicity-and quiet which goes together with it, because you can no longer believe in God, who is always appearing in it, then ask yourself if you have really lost God. Is it not much more, that you have never possessed Him? For when should that have been? Do you believe that children can contain Him, whom men can only bear with labour and the burden of whom weighs down the grey-haired? Do you believe that he, who possesses Him, could lose Him like a little stone, or do you not rather think with me that he who had Him, could only be lost by Him? But if you come to realise, that He did not exist in your childhood, nor beforehand; if you suspect that Christ was deceived by his yearning and Mohammed betrayed by his pride—if you feel with horror, that now in this hour in which we speak of Him He does not exist—what entitles you then to regret as a dead man Him who never existed, and to seek Him as if He had been lost?

Why do you not think that He is He who is coming, who from eternity has been at hand, the being of the future, the final fruit of a tree whose leaves we are? What keeps you from putting His birth into the times of the future and living your life as a painful but beautiful day in the history of a mighty pregnancy? For do you not see that everything that happens is ever beginning, and would it not be His beginning, since beginning is in itself always so beautiful? If He is the most complete, must not smaller things exist before Him, so that He can choose from plenteousness and superfluity? Must He not be the last in order to grasp everything to Himself? And what meaning would our lives have, if He for whom we are longing had already been?

As the bees bring together their honey, so do we take the sweetest from everything and build Him. Even with what is slight and unpretentious, as long as it comes to pass out of love, we begin; with work and with rest after work, with a silence of a little lovely joy, with everything that we do without participation or followers, we begin to form Him, whom we shall no more experience than our forefathers could experience us. Yet they are in us, those long-departed, as potentialities, as a burden upon our fate, as blood that flows murmuring in us, and as a countenance, that rises from out of the depths of time.

Is there anything that can take from you this hope some day to be in Him, at any rate in the furthest and uttermost part of Him?

Celebrate Christmas in this holy feeling, that perhaps He needs this very anxiety for life from you, in order to begin. These very days of your transition, when everything in you is working at Him, are perhaps just the same as those when as a child you worked breathlessly at Him. Be patient and without vexation, and remember that the least we can do is not to make His coming into being more difficult for Him than the earth makes it for the spring, when it wishes to come.

Be joyful and of good hope,

Yours,

Rainer Maria Rilke.

Letter Seven

My dear Herr Kappus,

It is a long time since I received your last letter, but do not hold that against me. First work, then troubles and finally ill-health, have been keeping me from this answer, which, as I wished it, was to come to you from good peaceful days. Now I feel somewhat better—here, too, I was affected by the beginning of spring with its evil, ill-humoured transitions—and now I manage, dear Herr Kappus, to greet you, as I am so heartily glad to do, and to tell you to the best of my ability one or two things concerning your letter.

You see, I have copied out your sonnet, because I considered it to be beautiful and simple and born in the form in which it runs with so much quiet grace. It is the best of your verses that I have been permitted to read. And now I give you that copy, because I know that it is important and makes for new experience to find one's own work again in someone else's hand-writing. Read the verses as if they were someone else's, and you will feel in your innermost being how utterly they are your own.

It has been a joy to me to read, again and again, this sonnet and your letter. I thank you for both of them.

And you must not be led astray in your loneliness, because there is something in you that desires to come out of you. If you think of it quietly and use it as an instrument, this very desire will help you to extend your loneliness over the broad lands. With the help of conventions, people have solved all problems according to what is easy and according to the easiest side of what is easy, but it is clear that we must attach ourselves to what is difficult. All living things attach themselves to it, everything in nature grows and defends itself after its manner and is an entity in itself, and strives to be so at any price and against all resistance. We know little, but that we must attach ourselves to what is difficult is a certainty that never deserts us. It is good to be lonely, for loneliness is difficult. The fact that a thing is difficult must be for us the more reason for doing it.

To love, too, is good, for love is difficult. Loving between human being and human being, that is perhaps the most difficult thing with which we have been charged, the extreme possibility, the last test and trial, the work for which all other work is but preparation. Wherefore young people, who are beginners in everything, do not yet know how to love: they must learn. With their whole being, with all their strength collected about their lonely, timid, upward straining hearts they must learn to love. Apprenticeship always a long time of seclusion, and so love, too, is for a long time right far into life, just loneliness, increased and deepened solitude for him who loves. Love is not at first anything that can be called merging or surrender or union with another, for what would the union be of what is unclean, unready, and still subordinate? It is an exalted occasion for the individual to ripen, to become something in himself, to become a world, to become a world in himself for another's sake; it is a great and even arrogant claim upon him, something that chooses him out and calls him to what is far. Only in this sense, as a duty to work at themselves ["to hearken and to hammer day and night"] should young people use the love that is given to them. Surrender and sacrifice and every kind of fusion is not for them, who must save up and collect a long, long time yet; it is that which comes at last, that perhaps, for which a life-time is still hardly sufficient.

But it is in this that young people go so often and so badly astray. It is in their nature to have no patience, so they throw themselves together when love comes over them, and spend themselves just as they are in all their disorder, confusion and perplexity. What is to happen then? What is life to do with the heaps of half-battered life, which they call their fusion, and which, if possible, they would gladly call their happiness and their future? Each one loses himself for the other's sake and loses the other, too, and many others who wanted to come afterwards. And each loses the immensity of his possibilities, and exchanges the coming and going of delicate things full of portent for a fruitless perplexity, of which nothing more can come; nothing but a little nausea, disappointment, poverty and flight into one of the many conventions which have been set up in great numbers like public shelters on this most dangerous of paths. No sphere of human experience is so well provided with conventions as this. Life-belts of the most different devices are there, boats and air-bladders. The conception of society has been able to create all kinds of refuges, for, as it was inclined to take the life of love as a pleasure, it had to make it easy, cheap, secure and safe, as public pleasures always are.

It is true that many young men, who have a false love—that is to say one that surrenders itself and is not lonely—and that is where the average will always remain—feel the oppression of a transgression and want to make the circumstance in which they find themselves capable of life and fruitful after their own personal manner. For nature tells them that the problems of love are less than anything else of importance, capable of a public solution according to some convention or other, that there are problems, intimate problems between one human being and another, which in each case need a new, a particular and a personal answer. But having already thrown themselves together, they no longer recognise any boundaries or any distinction between each other, and therefore have no longer any possessions of their own, so how should they be able, out of their own selves, out of the depth of their loneliness, to find a way out?

They act in common helplessness, and, even if with the best intention they want to avoid the convention—perhaps marriage—which opens itself to them, they fall into the clutches of another conventional solution, which may be less public, but which is just as deadly; that is all that surrounds them far and wide—convention; for, when it is a question of a troubled union which has been formed early, every treatment is conventional; every situation, to which such confusion leads, has its convention, however unusual, that is to say, however immoral in the ordinary sense of the word it may be; yes, even separation would then be a conventional step, an impersonal and chance decision without force and without fruit.

He, who considers it seriously, finds that as for death, which is difficult, so for love, which is difficult, too, no explanation or solution, no hint or path has yet been found out; and for these two charges, which we carry covered up and hand on afterwards without opening them, no common rule based on an agreement can possibly be discovered. But in proportion as we begin to try to live as individuals, so will these great things come nearer to meet us as individuals. The claims which the difficult task of love lays upon our development are beyond the possibilities of our life, and as beginners we are not yet equal to them. But if we endure and take this love upon ourselves as a burden and apprenticeship instead of losing ourselves in all the easy and thoughtless play, behind which men have hidden themselves in the presence of the most serious of the serious things of their existence, then those, who come long after us, will perhaps feel the effects of a little progress and a little alteration; which would be a great deal.

We are actually the first to come to the point of considering objectively and without prejudice the relationship of one individual human being to another, and in our attempts to live such a relationship we have no model before us, and yet there has already come to pass much in the course of time to help us in our timid beginnings.

In their new personal development the girl and the woman will only be for a short time imitations of the good and bad manners of man and reiterations of man's professions. After the uncertainty of this transition it will appear that women have passed through those many, often ridiculous, changes of disguise, only to free themselves from the disturbing influence of the other sex. For women, in whom life tarries and dwells in a more incommunicable, fruitful and confident form, must at bottom have become richer beings, more ideally human beings than fundamentally easy-going man, who is not drawn down beneath the surface of life by the difficulty of bearing bodily fruit, and who arrogantly and hastily undervalues what he means to love. When this humanity of woman, borne to the full in pain and humiliation, has stripped off in the course of the changes of its outward position the old convention of simple feminine weakness, it will come to light, and man, who cannot yet feel it coming, will be surprised and smitten by it. One day—a day of which trustworthy signs are already speaking and shining forth especially in northern lands—one day that girl and woman will exist, whose name will no longer mean simply a contrast to what is masculine, but something for itself, something that will not make one think of any supplement or limit, but only of life and existence—the feminine human beings.

This advance, at first very much against the will of man who has been overtaken—will alter the experience of love, which is now full of error, will change it radically and form it into a relationship, no longer between man and woman, but between human being and human being. And this more human love, which will be carried out with infinite consideration and gentleness and will be good and clean in its tyings and untyings, will be like that love which we are straining and toiling to prepare, the love which consists in this, that two lonely beings protect one another, border upon one another and greet one another.

Just this much more: do not think that that great love, which was entrusted to you as a boy, has been lost. Can you tell, whether great and good wishes did not ripen within you at that time and resolutions on which you still live to-day? I believe that that love lives so strongly and powerfully in your memory because it was your first deep solitude and the first inner work which you did at your own life. All good wishes to you, dear Herr Kappus!

Yours,

Rainer Maria Rilke.

Letter Eight

Borgeby Gård, Flådie, Sweden,

12th August, 1904

I should like to talk to you again for a little while, though I can say hardly anything that will be helpful and but little that will be useful. You have had many great sorrows, which have passed. And you say that this their passing, too, was difficult and discordant for you. But I beg you to consider whether these griefs have not rather gone right through you? Whether there has not been much change within you; whether, while you were sad, you did not alter in some point or other of your being? Only those sorrows are dangerous and bad which one carries with one to the company of other men in order to drown them. Like illnesses, which are superficially and badly treated, they only retreat into the background and break out again after a short interval worse than ever. They collect in one's innermost being and are life, unlived, rejected, lost life of which one can die. If it were possible for us to see a little further than our knowledge can reach, to see out a little farther over the outworks of our surmising, we should perhaps bear our griefs with greater confidence than our joys. For they are the moments when something new, something unknown enters into us. Our feelings are dumb with embarrassed shyness and everything in us retreats into the background. A stillness grows up, and the new thing, that nobody knows, stands in the middle of it and is silent.

I believe that nearly all our griefs are moments of suspense, which we experience as paralysis, because we can no longer hear our estranged feelings living. Because we are alone with that foreign thing, which has entered into us; because everything in which we have confidence and to which we are accustomed is for a moment taken away from us; because we are in the midst of a state of transition, in which we cannot remain. The grief, too, passes. The new thing in us, that which has been added to us, has entered into our heart and penetrated to its innermost chamber, and is no longer there even—it is already in our blood. We do not experience what it was. We could easily be made to believe that nothing had happened, and yet we have changed just as a house changes into which a guest has entered. We cannot say who has come and perhaps we shall never know, but there are many signs to assure us that the future enters into us in this way, so as to transform itself in us long before it happens. And this is why it is so important to be alone and attentive, when one is sad; because the apparently eventless and motionless moment, when our future enters into us, is so much nearer to life than that other manifestly chance point of time, when it actually happens to us as if from without. The quieter, the more patient, the more open we are in our grief, the deeper and the more unerringly does the new thing enter into us, the better do we make it our own, and the more does it become our fate; and when some day it happens [that is to say, when it passes out of us to others], we will feel ourselves in our innermost being related and near to it. And that is necessary. It is necessary—and this is the direction that our development gradually takes—that nothing strange to us should fall to our lot, but only that which has been in us for a long time. Men have already had to change their conceptions of many processes, and they will gradually come to realise that what we call fate comes out of human beings themselves and does not come upon them from without. It is only because so many did not absorb their fate while it lived in them, and did not make it into part of themselves, that they did not recognise what was coming out of them. It was so strange to them, that in their confused terror, they thought it must just that moment have come upon them, for they could take their oath that they have never found anything similar to it in themselves. Even as men long deceived themselves over the movement of the sun, so are they still deceiving themselves over the movement of what is to come. The future stands fast, Herr Kappus, but we are moving in infinite space. How should we not find it difficult?

And if we speak once more of loneliness, it becomes even clearer that that is not a thing which one can choose or reject. We are lonely. One can deceive oneself over it and behave as if it were not so. That is all. But how much better it is to realise that we are lonely and candidly to make that realisation our starting point. It is, of course, certain to make us giddy; for all the points upon which our eyes used to rest are taken away from us, there is no longer anything near to us, and that which is distant is infinitely distant. A man who had been transported from his room, with hardly any preparation or transition, to the peak of a great mountain, would be bound to have a similar feeling, a feeling of insecurity without parallel, a feeling of abandonment to nameless powers would almost annihilate him. He would imagine that he was falling or would believe that he had been hurled out into space or that he had burst asunder into a thousand fragments. What monstrous lies his brain would have to invent in order to come up with the situation of his senses and explain it! In like manner do all distances and all measures alter for him who becomes lonely. Of these changes many may happen suddenly, and then as with the man on the mountain-top, there arise strange fancies and unusual feelings, which seem to become greater than he can bear. But it is necessary for us to experience that, too. We must accept existence as far as ever it is possible. Everything, even the most unheard of things, must be possible in it. That is in fact the only kind of courage that is demanded of us—to be courageous in face of the strangest, the most astounding and the most inexplicable thing that can confront us. The fact that mankind has been cowardly in this sense has done infinite harm to life, for the experiences which men call "phenomena," the so-called "world of spirits," death—all these things that are so closely related to us, have been so thoroughly crowded out of life by man's daily self-defence, that the senses with which we could grasp them have become stunted. Let us not speak of God. But the anxiety men feel before the inexplicable has not only impoverished the existence of the individual. Through it the relations of human being to human being have been limited, lifted as it were from a river-bed of infinite possibilities on to a fallow bank, to which nothing happens. For it is not only laziness that brings it about that human relationships repeat themselves from one occasion to the next with such unspeakable monotony and staleness, but it is also shyness of any new experience whose end cannot be foreseen, to which men do not think they are equal. But only he who is prepared for everything and does not exclude anything, even the most enigmatical, will live his relationships with another as something really living and with himself get right to the bottom of his own existence. For, if we think of this existence of the individual as a room—be it large or small—it is evident that most people only get to know a corner of their room, a corner by the window, a strip on which they walk up or down. In this way they have a certain security: yet far more human is that perilous insecurity which drives the prisoners in Poe's stories to take hold of the shapes of their fearful prison and not to be strangers unfamiliar with the unspeakable horrors of their sojourn there. But we are not prisoners, no traps or snares are set around us and there is nothing that should frighten us or torment us. We have been sent into life as being the element to which we most nearly correspond, and, moreover, through thousands of years of adaptation to this life, we have become so like it that, when we stay still, through a happy mimicry we are hardly distinguishable from everything that surrounds us. We have no reason to be mistrustful towards our world, for it is not against us. If it has horrors, they are our horrors, if it has precipices, those precipices are ours, and, if there are dangers there, we must try to love them. And if we adjust our life to the principle which advises us that we must always attach ourselves to what is difficult, then that which now still appears to us most strange, will become our most familiar and loyal friend. How can we forget that old myth, which is to be found at the beginning of all peoples—the myth of the dragon, which at the last moment changes into a princess? Perhaps all the dragons of your life are princesses, who are only waiting for us to show a little beauty and courage. Perhaps at very bottom every horror is something helpless, that wants help from us.

And so, my dear Herr Kappus, you must not be horrified, if a grief rises up before you greater than any you have seen before. If over your hands and all your doings there passes an uneasiness, like light and cloud-shadows, you must bethink yourself, that something is happening to you, that life has not forgotten you, that it is holding you in its hands, and will not let you fall. Why do you want to exclude any disturbance, any woe or sadness from your life, seeing that you do not know what work their presence is performing in yourself? Why do you want to persecute yourself with the question, whence has come all that and whither is it going? Seeing that you know that you are in a state of transition and there is nothing you could desire more than to transform yourself. If something in your present life is sickly, remember that sickness is the means by which an organism frees itself of foreign elements. Then one must just help it to be sick, to have its sickness in its entirety and to let it come right out, for that is its means of progress. So much is happening in you now, dear Herr Kappus, that you must be patient like a sick man and confident like a convalescent, for perhaps you are both these two. And you are still more, you are also the doctor, who must watch over himself. But in every sickness there are many days when the doctor can do nothing but wait, and that is above all what you must do now, in so far as you are your own doctor.

Do not watch yourself too closely, do not be too quick to draw conclusions from that which is happening to you. Simply let it happen, otherwise you will come too easily to look, reproachfully—that is to say, from a moral point of view—upon your past, which naturally takes part in everything that is happening to you now. But what you remember and condemn is not that part of the confusions, desires, and yearnings of your boyhood which is effective within you. The extraordinary circumstances of a lonely and helpless childhood are so difficult and complicated, exposed to so many influences and at the same time so cut off from any really coherent scheme of life, that, when a vice enters into it, one cannot simply speak of it as vice. One must always be so careful with names; it is often by the name of a crime that a life is shattered and not by the nameless and personal action itself, which was. probably a perfectly definite necessity of that life and could without difficulty be accepted by it as such. The consumption of strength only seems to you to be so great, because you over-estimate the victory; it is not the victory that is the "great thing" you think you have performed, although you are right in your feeling. The great thing is this, that there was already something there which you could put in the place of that deception, something true and real. Without that your victory would only have been a moral reaction without any further meanings: as it is it has become an epoch in your life—your life, dear Herr Kappus, of which I think with so many good wishes. Do you remember how this life of yours yearned to pass out of childhood, and come to the state of "a big man"? I can see that it is now longing to leave the "big man" for the "bigger man." Therefore it does not cease to be difficult, but for that very reason it will also not cease to grow.

And if I am to say one thing more to you, it is this: do not believe that he who is trying to console you lives without troubles among the simple and quiet words which often do you good. His life is full of troubles and griefs and is not to be compared with yours. Were it not so, he could never have been able to find those words.

Yours,

Rainer Maria Rilke

Letter Nine

My dear Herr Kappus,

During this time, that has passed without a letter from me, I have been partly travelling and partly so busy, that I could not write. To-day, too, I find it difficult to write, because I have already had to write so many letters that my hand is tired. If I could dictate, I would say a great deal to you, but as it is you must take a few words only for your long letter.

I think of you often, and with good wishes so concentrated upon you that I am sure it must somehow have helped you. I often doubt whether my letters can really be a help to you. Do not say: "Yes, they are." Accept them quietly and without much thanks, and let us wait and see what will come of them. It is perhaps useless for me to go into your words in detail, for what I could say about your tendency to doubts and your inability to harmonise your outward and inward life, or about anything else that is afflicting you, is always the same as what I have already said; the wish that you may find enough patience in yourself to endure, and enough simplicity, to believe, that you may gain more and more confidence in that which is difficult, and in your loneliness among other men. And for the rest let life happen to you. Believe me, life is right in every case.

Concerning feelings: all these feelings are pure which comprehend your whole being and lift it up; impure is the feeling that only grasps one side of your being and thus distorts you. All thoughts you can have with regard to your childhood are good. Everything that makes of you something more than you were beforehand in your best moments, is right. Every elation is good as long as it pervades your whole being, is not intoxication and confusion, but joy so clear that one can see to its very depth. Do you understand what I mean?

Your doubt can become a good quality if you educate it. It must gain knowledge and power of criticism. If it wants to destroy anything, ask it why that something is worthy of destruction: demand proofs from it, test it, and you will perhaps find that it is at a loss and embarrassed, perhaps even rebellious. But do not give in. Demand arguments and deal in this way attentively and consistently with each separate occasion, and the day will come, when instead of being destructive, it will become one of your best workers—perhaps the most skilful of all the workers, who are engaged in the building up of your life.

That is all I can say to you to-day. But I send you at the same time the copy of a little poem, which has now appeared in the Prague "German Work." There I speak further to you of life and death and of how both are great and powerful.

Rainer Maria Rilke

Letter Ten

Paris,

26th December, 1908.

You must know, dear Herr Kappus, how glad I was to get your beautiful letter. The news which you give me, tangible and substantial as it is once again, appears to me to be good, and the longer I thought of it, the more did I feel that it really was good. As a matter of fact I wanted to write this to you for Christmas Eve; but in the midst of the varied and uninterrupted work, in which I have spent this winter, the old festival came upon me so suddenly, that I hardly had time to attend to the most necessary matters, much less for writing letters.

But I have often thought of you during these festival days and have pictured to myself how quiet you must be in your lonely fort among the empty mountains, over which those mighty southern winds hurl themselves, as if they wanted to swallow them up in large pieces.

The stillness in which there is room for such noises and movements must be immense, and when one thinks that to all that is added the distant presence of the sea, joining in with its note, perhaps the innermost note in this prehistoric harmony, then one can only wish for you, that you may confidently and patiently let this mighty loneliness work upon you. Nothing will be able to strike it out of your life afterwards. In every experience and action that lies before you it will, as a nameless influence, have a continued and imperceptibly decisive effect upon you, something after the manner in which our forefathers' blood stirs unceasingly within us and joins itself to our own to form that unique and unrepeatable thing, that we ourselves are in all the changes of our life.

Yes, I rejoice that you have this solid, definite existence, the title and the uniform, the service and all those tangible and limited things, which, in such surroundings, in the company of a handful of men alike isolated, assume an earnestness and become a necessity, which above and beyond the game and pastime of a military career constitute an employment that demands vigilance, and which do not only leave room for, but actually themselves train an independent watchfulness. That we should be in situations, which work upon us and bring us from time to time face to face with the great things of nature—that is all that is necessary.

Art, too, is only a form of life, and by living in no matter what way one can be unconsciously preparing oneself for it; in every real career one is nearer to art and more its neighbour than in those unreal half-artistic careers, which pretend to be near to art, but in practice deny and attack the existence of all art—somewhat in the manner of all journalism and nearly all criticism, and three-quarters of what is and would like to be called literature. In a word I rejoice that you have overcome the danger of falling into those professions, and that somewhere in a hard reality you are lonely and courageous. May the year that lies before you keep you and strengthen you in it.

Ever yours,

R. M. Rilke

POEMS

Translated by **Jessie Lamont**

With an Introduction by **H.T.**

Acknowledgment

To the Editors of Poetry--A magazine of Verse, and Poet Lore, the translator is indebted for permission to reprint certain poems in this book--also to the compilers of the following anthologies--Amphora II edited by Thomas Bird Mosher--The Catholic Anthology of World Poetry selected by Carl van Doren.

CONTENTS

The Poetry Of Rainer Maria Rilke

The supreme problem of every age is that of finding its consummate artistic expression. Before this problem every other remains of secondary importance. History defines and directs its physical course, science cooperates in the achievement of its material aims, but Art alone gives to the age its spiritual physiognomy, its ultimate and lasting expression. The process of Art is on the one hand sensuous, the conception having for its basis the fineness of organization of the senses; and on the other hand it is severely scientific, the value of the creation being dependent upon the craftsmanship, the mastery over the tool, the technique. Art, like Nature, its great and only reservoir for all time past and all time to come, ever strives for elimination and selection. It is severe and aristocratic in the application of its laws and impervious to appeal to serve other than its own aims. Its purpose is the symbolization of Life. In its sanctum there reigns the silence of vast accomplishment, the serene, final, and imperturbable solitude which is the ultimate criterion of all great things created.

To speak of Poetry is to speak of the most subtle, the most delicate, and the most accurate instrument by which to measure Life.

Poetry is reality's essence visioned and made manifest by one endowed with a perception acutely sensitive to sound, form, and colour, and gifted with a power to shape into rhythmic and rhymed verbal symbols the reaction to Life's phenomena. The poet moulds that which appears evanescent and ephemeral in image and in mood into everlasting values. In this act of creation he serves eternity.

Poetry, in especial lyrical poetry, must be acknowledged the supreme art, culminating as it does in a union of the other arts, the musical, the plastic, and the pictorial.

The most eminent contemporary poets of Europe have, each in accordance with his individual temperament, reflected in their work the spiritual essence of our age, its fears and failures, its hopes and high achievements: Maeterlinck, with his mood of resignation and his retirement into a dusky twilight where his shadowy figures move noiselessly like phantoms in fate-laden dimness; Dehmel, the worshipper of will, with his passion for materiality and the beauty of all things physical and tangible; Verhaeren, the visionary of a new vitality, who sees in the toilers of fields and factories the heroic gesture of our time and who might have written its great epic of industry but for the overwhelming lyrical mood of his soul.

Until a few years ago, known only to a relatively small community on the continent but commanding an ever increasing attention which has borne his name far beyond the boundary of his country, the personality of Rainer Maria Rilke stands to-day beside the most illustrious poets of modern Europe.

*   *   *   *   *

The background against which the figure of Rainer Maria Rilke is silhouetted is so varied, the influences which have entered into his life are so manifold, that a study of his work, however slight, must needs take into consideration the elements through which this poet has matured into a great master.

Prague, the city in which Rilke was born in 1875, with its sinister palaces and crumbling towers that rose in the early Middle Ages and have reached out into our time like the threatening fingers of mighty hands which have wielded swords for generations and which are stained with the blood of many wounds of many races; the city where amid grey old ruins blonde maidens are at play or are lost in reverie in the green cool parks and shady gardens with which the Bohemian capital abounds, this Prague of mingled grotesqueness and beauty gave to the young boy his first impressions.

There is a period in the life of every artist when his whole being seems lost in a contemplation of the surrounding world, when the application to work is difficult, like the violent forcing of something that is awaiting its time. This is the time of his dream, as sacred as the days of early spring before wind and rain and light have touched the fruits of the fields, when there is a tense bleak silence over the whole of nature, in which is wrapped the strength of storms and the glow of the summer's sun. This is the time of his deepest dream, and upon this dream and its guarding depends the final realization of his life's work.

The young graduate of the Gymnasium was to enter upon the career of an army officer in accordance with the traditions of the family, an old noble house which traces its lineage far back to Carinthian ancestry. His inclinations, however, pointed so decisively in the direction of the finer arts of life that he left the Military Academy after a very short attendance to devote himself to the study of philosophy and the history of art.

As one turns the pages of Rilke's first small book of poems, published originally under the title Larenopfer, in the year 1895, and which appeared in more recent editions under the less descriptive name Erste Gedichte, one realizes at once, in spite of a lack of plasticity in the presentation, that here speaks one who has lingered long and lovingly over the dream of his boyhood. As the title indicates, these poems are a tribute, an offering to the Lares, the home spirits of his native town. Prague and the surrounding country are the ever recurring theme of almost every one of these poems. The meadows, the maidens, the dark river in the evening, the spires of the cathedral at night rising like grey mists are seen with a wonderment, the great well-spring of all poetic imagination, with a well-nigh religious piety. Through all these poems there sounds like a subdued accompaniment a note of gratitude for the ability to thus vision the world, to be sunk in the music of all things. "Without is everything that I feel within myself, and without and within myself everything is immeasurable, illimitable."

These pictures of town and landscape are never separated from their personal relation to the poet. He feels too keenly his dependence upon them, as a child views flowers and stars as personal possessions. Not until later was he to reach the height of an impersonal objectivity in his art. What distinguishes these early poems from similar adolescent productions is the restraint in the presentation, the economy and intensity of expression and that quality of listening to the inner voice of things which renders the poet the seer of mankind.

The second book of poems appeared two years later and like the first volume *Traumgekroent* is full of the music that is reminiscent of the mild melancholy of the Bohemian folk-songs, in whose gentle rhythms the barbaric strength of the race seems to be lulled to rest as the waves of a far-away tumultuous sea gently lap the shore. The themes of *Traumgekroent* are extended somewhat beyond the immediate environment of Prague and some of the most beautiful poems are luminous pictures of villages hidden in the snowy blossoming of May and June, out of which rises here and there the solitary soft voice of a boy or girl singing. In these first two volumes the poet is satisfied with painting in words, full of sonorous beauty, the surrounding world. From this period dates the small poem *Evening*, which seems to have been sketched by a Japanese painter, so clear and colourful is its texture, so precious and precise are its outlines.

With *Advent* and *Mir Zur Feier*, both published within the following three years, a phase of questioning commences, a dim desire begins to stir to reach out into the larger world "deep into life, out beyond time." Whereas the early poems were characterized by a tendency to turn away from the turmoil of life--in fact, the concrete world of reality does not seem to exist--there is noticeable in these two later volumes an advance toward life in the sense that the poet is beginning to approach and to vision some of its greatest symbols.

Throughout the entire work of Rilke, in his poetry as well as in his interpretations of painting and sculpture, there are two elements that constitute the cornerstones in the structure of his art. If, as has been said with a degree of verity, Nietzsche was primarily a musician whose philosophy had for its basis and took its ultimate aspects from the musical quality of his artistic endowment, it may be maintained with an equal amount of truth that Rilke is primarily a painter and sculptor whose poetry rests upon the fundaments of the pictorial and plastic arts.

Up to the time of the publication of these volumes, Rilke's poems possessed a quietude, a stillness suggested in the straight unbroken yet delicate lines of the picture which he portrays and in the soft, almost unpulsating rhythm of his words. The approach of evening or nightfall, the coming of dawn, the change of the seasons, the slow changes of light into darkness and of darkness into light, in short, the most silent yet greatest metamorphoses in the external aspects of nature form the contents of many of these first poems. The inanimate object and the living creature in nature are not seen in the sharp contours of their isolation; they are viewed and interpreted in the atmosphere that surrounds them, in which they are enwrapped and so densely veiled that the outlines are only dimly visible, be that atmosphere the mystic grey of northern twilight or the dark velvety blue of southern summer nights. In *Advent*, the experience of the atmosphere becomes an experience in his innermost soul and, therefore, all things become of value to him only in so far as they partake of the atmosphere, as they are seen in a peculiar air and distance. This first phase in Rilke's work may be defined as the phase of reposeful nature.

To this sphere of relaxation and restfulness in which the objects are static and are changed only as the surrounding atmosphere affects them, the second phase in the poet's development adds another element, which later was to grow into dimensions so powerful, so violently breaking beyond the limitations of simple expression in words that it could only find its satisfaction in a dithyrambic hymn to the work of the great plastic artist of our time, to the creations of Auguste Rodin. This second element is that which the French sculptor in a different medium has carried to perfection. It is the element of gesture, of dramatic movement.

This might seem the appropriate place in which to speak of Rilke's monograph on the art of Rodin. To do so would, however, be an undue anticipation, for it will be necessary to trace Rilke's development through several transitions before the value of his contact with the work of Rodin can be fully measured.

The gesture, the movement begins in *Advent* and *Celebration* to disturb the stillness prevailing in the first two volumes of poems. Even here it is only gentle and shy at first like the stirring of a breath of wind over a quiet sea; and gentle beings make this first gesture, children and young women at play, singing, dancing or at prayer.

Particularly in the cycle *Songs of the Maidens* in the book *Celebration*, the atmosphere is condensed and becomes the psychic background of the landscape against which the gesture of longing or expectation is seen and felt. It is the impatience to burst into blossoming, the longing for love which pulsates in these *Songs of the Maidens* with the tenseness of suspense. *The Prayers of the Maidens to Mary* have not the mild melody of maidenly prayer; they vibrate with the ecstasy of expectant life, and the Madonna is more than the Heavenly Virgin, their longing transforms her into the symbol of earthly love and motherhood. This expectation, in spite of its intensity, is subdued and is only heard like the cadence of a far off dream:

"How shall I go on tiptoe From childhood to Annunciation Through the dim twilight Into Thy Garden?"

Mention should be made of some prose writings which Rilke published in the year 1898 and shortly afterward. They are *Two Stories of Prague, The Touch of Life* and *The Last*; three volumes of short stories; a two-act drama, *The Daily Life*, points to a strong Maeterlinck influence, and finally *Stories of God*. With both beauty of detail and problematic interest, the short stories show an incoherence of treatment and a lack of dramatic co-ordination easily conceivable in a poet who is essentially lyrical and who at that time had not mastered the means of technique to give to his characters the clear chiselling of the epic form.

*   *   *   *   *

A sojourn in Russia and especially the acquaintance with the novels of Dostoievsky became potent factors in Rilke's development and served to deepen creations which without this influence might have terminated in a grandiose aesthesia.

Broadly speaking, Russian art and literature may be described as springing from an ethical impulse and as having for their motive power and *raison d'etre* the tendency toward socio-political reform, in contradistinction to the art and literature of Western culture, whose motives and aims are primarily of an aesthetic nature and seek in art the reconciliation of the dualism between spirit and matter.

Dostoievsky, whom Merejkovsky describes somewhere as the man with the never-young face, the face "with its shadows of suffering and its wrinkles of sunken-in cheeks ... but that which gives to this face its most tortured expression is its seeming immobility, the suddenly interrupted impulse, the life hardened into a stone:" this Dostoievsky and particularly his *Rodion Raskolnikov* cycle became a profound artistic experience to Rilke. The poor, the outcasts, the homeless ones received for him a new significance, the significance of the isolated figure placed in the mighty everchanging current of a life in which this figure stands strong and solitary. In the poem entitled *Pont Du Carrousel*, written in Paris a few years later, Rilke has visioned the blind beggar aloof amid the fluctuating crowds of the metropolis.

Of Russia and its influence upon him, Rilke writes: "Russia became for me the reality and the deep daily realization that reality is something that comes infinitely slowly to those who have patience. Russia is the country where men are solitary, each one with a world within himself, each one profound in his humbleness and without fear of humiliating himself, and because of that truly pious. Here the words of men are only fragile bridges above their real life."

The great symbols of Solitude and of Death enter into the poet's work.

*   *   *   *   *

In the first decade of the new century Rilke reached the height of his art and with a few exceptions the poems represented in this volume are selected from the poems which were published between the years 1900 and 1908. The ascent toward the acme of Rilke's art after the year 1900 is as rapid as it is precipitous. Only a few years previous we read in Advent:

"That is longing: To dwell in the flux of things, To have no home in the present. And these are wishes: gentle dialogues Of the poor hours with eternity."

With *Das Buch der Bilder* the dream is ended, the veil of mist is lifted and before us are revealed pictures and images that rise before our eyes in clear colourful contours. Whether the poet conjures from the depths of myth *The Kings in Legends*, or whether we read from *The Chronicle of a Monk* the awe-inspiring description of *The Last Judgment Day*, or whether in Paris on a Palm Sunday we see *The Maidens at Confirmation*, the pictures presented stand out with the clearness and finality of the typical.

It is a significant fact that Rilke dedicated this book to Gerhart Hauptmann, "in love and gratitude for his Michael Kramer." Hauptmann, like Rilke in these poems, has placed before us great epic figures and his art is so concentrated that often the simple expression of the thought of one of his characters produces a shudder in the listener or reader because in this thought there vibrates the suffering of an entire social class and in it resounds the sorrow of many generations.

* * * * *

In *The Book of Pictures*, Rilke's art reaches its culmination on what might be termed its monumental side. The visualization is elevated to the impersonal objective level which gives to the rhythm of these poems an imperturbable calm, to the figures presented a monumental erectness. *The Men of the House of Colonna, The Czars, Charles XII Riding Through the Ukraine* are portrayed each with his individual historical gesture, with a luminosity as strong as the colour and movement which they gave to their time. In the mythical poem, *Kings in Legends*, this concrete element in the art of Rilke has found perhaps its supreme expression:

"Kings in old legends seem
Like mountains rising in the evening light.
They blind all with their gleam,
Their loins encircled are by girdles bright,
Their robes are edged with bands
Of precious stones--the rarest earth affords--
With richly jeweled hands
They hold their slender, shining, naked swords."

There are in *The Book of Pictures* poems in which this will to concentrate a mood into its essence and finality is applied to purely lyrical poems as in *Initiation*, that stands out in this volume like "the great dark tree" itself so immeasurable is the straight line of its aspiration reaching into the far distant silence of the night; or as in the poem entitled *Autumn*, with its melancholy mood of gentle descent in all nature.

In *The Book of Hours*, Rilke withdraws from the world not from weariness but weighed down under the manifold conflicting visions. As the prophet who would bring to the world a great possession must go forth into the desert to be alone until the kingdom comes to him from within, so the poet must leave the world in order to gain the deeper understanding, to be face to face with God. The mood of *Das Stunden-Buch* is this mood of being face to face with God; it elevates these poems to prayer, profound prayer of doubt and despair, exalted prayer of reconciliation and triumph.

The Book of Hours contains three parts written at different periods in the poet's life: *The Book of a Monk's Life* (1899); *The Book of Pilgrimage* (1901), and *The Book of Poverty and Death* (1903), although the entire volume was not published until several years later. *The Book of Hours* glows with a mystic fervour to know God, to be near him. In this desire to approach the Nameless One, the young Brother in *The Book of a Monk's Life* builds up about God parables, images and legends reminiscent of those of the 17th century Angelus Silesius, but sustained by a more pregnant language because exalted by a more ardent visionary force. The motif of *The Monk's Life* is expressed in the poem beginning with the lines:

"I live my life in circles that grow wide   And endlessly unroll."

Through the grey cell of the young Monk there flash in luminous magnificence the colours of the great renaissance masters, for he feels in Titian, in Michelangelo, in Raphael the same fervour that animates him; they, too, are worshippers of the same God.

There are poems in *The Book of Pilgrimage* of the stillness of a whispered prayer in a great Cathedral and there are others that carry in their exultation the music of mighty hymns. The visions in this second book are no less ecstatic though less glowingly colourful; they have withdrawn inward and have brought a great peace and a great faith as in the poem of God, whose very manifestation is the quietude and hush of a silent world:

"By day Thou art the Legend and the Dream
That like a whisper floats about all men,
The deep and brooding stillnesses which seem,
After the hour has struck, to close again.
And when the day with drowsy gesture bends
And sinks to sleep beneath the evening skies,
As from each roof a tower of smoke ascends
So does Thy Realm, my God, around me rise."

The last part of *The Book of Hours*, *The Book of Poverty and Death*, is finally a symphony of variations on the two great symbolic themes in the work of Rilke. As Christ in the parable of the rich young man demands the abandonment of all treasures, so in this book the poet sees the coming of the Kingdom, the fulfilment of all our longings for a nearness to God when we have become simple again like little children and poor in possessions like God Himself. In this phase of Rilke's development, the principle of renunciation constitutes a certain negative element in his philosophy. The poet later proceeded to a positive acquiescence toward man's possessions, at least those acquired or created in the domain of art.

In our approach through the mystic we touch reality most deeply. It is because of this that all art and all philosophy culminate in their final forms in a crystallization of those values of life that remain forever inexplicable to pure reason; they become religious in the simple, profound sense of that word. Before the eternal facts of Life doubt and strife are reconciled into faith, will and pride change into humility. The realization of this truth expressed in the medium of poetry is the significance of Rilke's *Book of Hours*. A distinguished Scandinavian writer has pronounced *Das Stunden-Buch* one of the supreme literary achievements of our time and its deepest and most beautiful book of prayer.

In his subsequent poetic work Rilke did not again reach the sustained high quality of this book, the mood and idea of which he incorporated into a prose work of exquisite lyrical beauty: *The Sketch of Malte Laurids Brigge*.

*   *   *   *   *

In *New Poems* (1907) and *New Poems, Second Part* (1908) the historical figure, frequently taken from the Old Testament, has grown beyond the proportions of life; it is weightier with fate and invariably becomes the means of expressing symbolically an abstract thought or a great human destiny. *Abishag* presents the contrast between the dawning and the fading life; *David Singing Before Saul* shows the impatience of awakening ambition, and *Joshua* is the man who forces even God to do his will. The antique Hellenic world rises with shining splendour in the poems *Eranna to Sappho, Lament for Antinous, Early Apollo* and the *Archaic Torso of Apollo*.

The spirit of the Middle Ages with its religious fervour and superstitious fanaticism is symbolized in several poems, the most important among which are *The Cathedral, God in the Middle Ages, Saint Sebastian* personifying martyrdom, and *The Rose Window*, whose glowing magic is compared to the hypnotic power of the tiger's eye. Modern Paris is often the background of the *New Poems*, and the crass play of light and shadow upon the waxen masks of Life's disillusioned in the Morgue is caught with the same intense realistic vision as the flamingos and parrots spreading their vari-coloured soft plumage in the warmth of the sun in the Avenue of the Jardin des Plantes.

Almost all of the poems in these two volumes are short and precise. The images are portrayed with the sensitive intensity of impressionistic technique. The majestic quietude of the long lines of *The Book of Pictures* is broken, the colours are more vibrant, more scintillating and the pictures are painted in nervous, darting strokes as though to convey the manner in which they were perceived: in one single, all-absorbing glance. For this reason many of these *New Poems* are not quite free from a certain element of virtuosity. On the other hand, Rilke achieves at times a perfect surety of rapid stroke as in the poem *The Spanish Dancer*, who rises luminously on the horizon of our inner vision like a circling element of fire, flaming and blinding in the momentum of her movements. Degas and Zuloaga seem to have combined their art on one canvas to give to this dancer the abundant elasticity of grace and the splendid fantasy of colour.

* * * * *

Many of the themes in the *New Poems* bear testimony to the fact that Rilke travelled extensively, prior to the writing of these volumes, in Italy, Germany, France, and Scandinavia. His book on the five painters at the artists' colony at Worpswede, where he remained for a time, entirely given over to the observation of the atmosphere, the movement of the sky and the play of light upon the far heath of this northern landscape, is an introduction to every interpretation of the work of landscape painters and a tender poem to a land whose solitary and melancholy beauty entered into his own work.

More vital than the influence of the personalities and

the art treasures of the countries which Rilke visited and more potent in its effect upon his creations, like a great sun over the most fruitful years of his life, stands the towering personality of Auguste Rodin. The *New Poems* bear the dedication: "A mon grand ami, Auguste Rodin," indicating the twofold influence which the French sculptor wielded over the poet, that of a friend and that of an artist.

One recalls the broad, solidly-built figure of Rodin with his rugged features and high, finely chiselled forehead, moving slowly among the white glistening marble busts and statues as a giant in an old legend moves among the rocks and mountains of his realm, patient, all-enduring, the man who has mastered life, strong and tempered by the storms of time. And one thinks of Rainer Maria Rilke, young, blond, with his slender aristocratic figure, the slightly bent-forward figure of one who on solitary walks meditates much and intensely, with his sensitive full mouth and the "firm structure of the eyebrow gladly sunk in the shadow of contemplation," the face full of dreams and with an expression of listening to some distant music.

From no other book of his, not excepting *The Book of Hours*, can we deduce so accurate a conception of Rilke's philosophy of Life and Art as we can draw from his comparatively short monograph on Auguste Rodin.

Rilke sees in Rodin the dominant personification in our age of the "power of servitude in all nature." For this reason the book on Rodin is far more than a purely aesthetic valuation of the sculptor's work; Rilke traces throughout the book the strongly ethical principle which works itself out in every creative act in the realm of art. This grasp of the deeper significance of all art gives to the book on Rodin its well-nigh religious aspect of thought and its hymnlike rhythm of expression. He begins: "Rodin was solitary before fame came to him, and afterward he became perhaps still more solitary. For fame is ultimately but the summary of all misunderstandings that crystallize about a new name." And he sums up this one man's greatness: "Sometime it will be realized what has made this great artist so supreme. He was a worker whose only desire was to penetrate with all his forces into the humble and the difficult significance of his tool. Therein lay a certain renunciation of life but in just this renunciation lay his triumph--for Life entered into his work."

Rodin became to Rilke the manifestation of the divine principle of the creative impulse in man. Thus Rilke's monograph on Auguste Rodin will remain the poet's testament on Life and Art.

*   *   *   *   *

Rilke has lived deeply; he has absorbed into his artistic and spiritual consciousness many of the supreme values of our time. His art holds the mystic depth of the Slav, the musical strength of the German, and the visual clarity of the Latin. As artist, he has felt life to be sacred, and as a priest, he has brought to its altar many offerings.

H.T.

NEW YORK CITY,
AUTUMN, 1918

FIRST POEMS

EVENING

The bleak fields are asleep,
My heart alone wakes;
The evening in the harbour
Down his red sails takes.

Night, guardian of dreams,
Now wanders through the land;
The moon, a lily white,
Blossoms within her hand.

MARY VIRGIN

How came, how came from out thy night
Mary, so much light
And so much gloom:
Who was thy bridegroom?

Thou callest, thou callest and thou hast forgot
That thou the same art not
Who came to me
In thy Virginity.

I am still so blossoming, so young.
How shall I go on tiptoe
From childhood to Annunciation
Through the dim twilight
Into thy Garden.

THE BOOK OF PICTURES

PRESAGING

I am like a flag unfurled in space,
I scent the oncoming winds and must bend with them,
While the things beneath are not yet stirring,
While doors close gently and there is silence in the chimneys
And the windows do not yet tremble and the dust is still
heavy--
Then I feel the storm and am vibrant like the sea
And expand and withdraw into myself
And thrust myself forth and am alone in the great storm.

AUTUMN

The leaves fall, fall as from far,
Like distant gardens withered in the heavens;
They fall with slow and lingering descent.

And in the nights the heavy Earth, too, falls
From out the stars into the Solitude.

Thus all doth fall. This hand of mine must fall
And lo! the other one:--it is the law.
But there is One who holds this falling
Infinitely softly in His hands.

SILENT HOUR

Whoever weeps somewhere out in the world
Weeps without cause in the world
Weeps over me.

Whoever laughs somewhere out in the night
Laughs without cause in the night
Laughs at me.

Whoever wanders somewhere in the world
Wanders in vain in the world
Wanders to me.

Whoever dies somewhere in the world
Dies without cause in the world
Looks at me.

THE ANGELS

They all have tired mouths
And luminous, illimitable souls;
And a longing (as if for sin)
Trembles at times through their dreams.

They all resemble one another,
In God's garden they are silent
Like many, many intervals
In His mighty melody.

But when they spread their wings
They awaken the winds
That stir as though God
With His far-reaching master hands
Turned the pages of the dark book of Beginning.

SOLITUDE

Solitude is like a rain
That from the sea at dusk begins to rise;
It floats remote across the far-off plain
Upward into its dwelling-place, the skies,
Then o'er the town it slowly sinks again.
Like rain it softly falls at that dim hour
When ghostly lanes turn toward the shadowy morn;
When bodies weighed with satiate passion's power
Sad, disappointed from each other turn;
When men with quiet hatred burning deep
Together in a common bed must sleep--
Through the gray, phantom shadows of the dawn
Lo! Solitude floats down the river wan ...

KINGS IN LEGENDS

Kings in old legends seem
Like mountains rising in the evening light.
They blind all with their gleam,
Their loins encircled are by girdles bright,
Their robes are edged with bands
Of precious stones--the rarest earth affords--
With richly jeweled hands
They hold their slender, shining, naked swords.

THE KNIGHT

The Knight rides forth in coat of mail
Into the roar of the world.
And here is Life: the vines in the vale
And friend and foe, and the feast in the hall,
And May and the maid, and the glen and the grail;
God's flags afloat on every wall
In a thousand streets unfurled.

Beneath the armour of the Knight
Behind the chain's black links
Death crouches and thinks and thinks:
"When will the sword's blade sharp and bright
Forth from the scabbard spring
And cut the network of the cloak
Enmeshing me ring on ring--
When will the foe's delivering stroke
Set me free
To dance
And sing?"

THE BOY

I wish I might become like one of these
Who, in the night on horses wild astride,
With torches flaming out like loosened hair
On to the chase through the great swift wind ride.
I wish to stand as on a boat and dare
The sweeping storm, mighty, like flag unrolled
In darkness but with helmet made of gold
That shimmers restlessly. And in a row,

Behind me in the dark, ten men that glow
With helmets that are restless, too, like mine,
Now old and dull, now clear as glass they shine.
One stands by me and blows a blast apace
On his great flashing trumpet and the sound
Shrieks through the vast black solitude around
Through which, as through a wild mad dream we race.
The houses fall behind us on their knees,
Before us bend the streets and them we gain,
The great squares yieled to us and them we seize--
And on our steeds rush like the roar of rain.

INITIATION

Whosoever thou art! Out in the evening roam,
Out from thy room thou know'st in every part,
And far in the dim distance leave thy home,
Whosoever thou art.
Lift thine eyes which lingering see
The shadows on the foot-worn threshold fall,
Lift thine eyes slowly to the great dark tree
That stands against heaven, solitary, tall,
And thou hast visioned Life, its meanings rise
Like words that in the silence clearer grow;
As they unfold before thy will to know
Gently withdraw thine eyes--

THE NEIGHBOUR

Strange violin! Dost thou follow me?
In many foreign cities, far away,
Thy lone voice spoke to me like memory.
Do hundreds play thee, or does but one play?

Are there in all great cities tempest-tossed
Men who would seek the rivers but for thee,

Who, but for thee, would be forever lost?
Why drifts thy lonely voice always to me?
Why am I the neighbour always
Of those who force to sing thy trembling strings?
Life is more heavy--thy song says--
Than the vast, heavy burden of all things.

SONG OF THE STATUE

Who so loveth me that he
Will give his precious life for me?
I shall be set free from the stone
If someone drowns for me in the sea,
I shall have life, life of my own,--
For life I ache.

I long for the singing blood,
The stone is so still and cold.
I dream of life, life is good.
Will no one love me and be bold
And me awake?

I weep and weep alone,
Weep always for my stone.
What joy is my blood to me
If it ripens like red wine?
It cannot call back from the sea
The life that was given for mine,
Given for Love's sake.

MAIDENS I

Others must by a long dark way
Stray to the mystic bards,
Or ask someone who has heard them sing
Or touch the magic chords.
Only the maidens question not
The bridges that lead to Dream;
Their luminous smiles are like strands of pearls
On a silver vase agleam.

The maidens' doors of Life lead out
Where the song of the poet soars,
And out beyond to the great world--
To the world beyond the doors.

MAIDENS II

Maidens the poets learn from you to tell
How solitary and remote you are,
As night is lighted by one high bright star
They draw light from the distance where you dwell.

For poet you must always maiden be
Even though his eyes the woman in you wake
Wedding brocade your fragile wrists would break,
Mysterious, elusive, from him flee.

Within his garden let him wait alone
Where benches stand expectant in the shade
Within the chamber where the lyre was played
Where he received you as the eternal One.

Go! It grows dark--your voice and form no more
His senses seek; he now no longer sees
A white robe fluttering under dark beech trees
Along the pathway where it gleamed before.

He loves the long paths where no footfalls ring,
And he loves much the silent chamber where
Like a soft whisper through the quiet air
He hears your voice, far distant, vanishing.

The softly stealing echo comes again
From crowds of men whom, wearily, he shuns;
And many see you there--so his thought runs--
And tenderest memories are pierced with pain.

THE BRIDE

Call me, Beloved! Call aloud to me!
Thy bride her vigil at the window keeps;
The evening wanes to dusk, the dimness creeps
Down empty alleys of the old plane-tree.

O! Let thy voice enfold me close about,
Or from this dark house, lonely and remote,
Through deep blue gardens where gray shadows float
I will pour forth my soul with hands stretched out ...

AUTUMNAL DAY

Lord! It is time. So great was Summer's glow:
Thy shadows lay upon the dials' faces
And o'er wide spaces let thy tempests blow.

Command to ripen the last fruits of thine,
Give to them two more burning days and press
The last sweetness into the heavy wine.

He who has now no house will ne'er build one,
Who is alone will now remain alone;
He will awake, will read, will letters write
Through the long day and in the lonely night;
And restless, solitary, he will rove
Where the leaves rustle, wind-blown, in the grove.

MOONLIGHT NIGHT

South-German night! the ripe moon hangs above
Weaving enchantment o'er the shadowy lea.
From the old tower the hours fall heavily
Into the dark as though into the sea--
A rustle, a call of night-watch in the grove,

Then for a while void silence fills the air;
And then a violin (from God knows where)
Awakes and slowly sings: Oh Love ... Oh Love ...

IN APRIL

Again the woods are odorous, the lark
Lifts on upsoaring wings the heaven gray
That hung above the tree-tops, veiled and dark,
Where branches bare disclosed the empty day.

After long rainy afternoons an hour
Comes with its shafts of golden light and flings
Them at the windows in a radiant shower,
And rain drops beat the panes like timorous wings.

Then all is still. The stones are crooned to sleep
By the soft sound of rain that slowly dies;
And cradled in the branches, hidden deep
In each bright bud, a slumbering silence lies.

MEMORIES OF A CHILDHOOD

The darkness hung like richness in the room
When like a dream the mother entered there
And then a glass's tinkle stirred the air
Near where a boy sat in the silent gloom.

The room betrayed the mother--so she felt--
She kissed her boy and questioned "Are you here?"
And with a gesture that he held most dear
Down for a moment by his side she knelt.

Toward the piano they both shyly glanced
For she would sing to him on many a night,
And the child seated in the fading light
Would listen strangely as if half entranced,

His large eyes fastened with a quiet glow
Upon the hand which by her ring seemed bent
And slowly wandering o'er the white keys went
Moving as though against a drift of snow.

DEATH

Before us great Death stands
Our fate held close within his quiet hands.
When with proud joy we lift Life's red wine
To drink deep of the mystic shining cup
And ecstasy through all our being leaps--
Death bows his head and weeps.

THE ASHANTEE
(Jardin d'Acclimatation, Paris)

No vision of exotic southern countries,
No dancing women, supple, brown and tall
Whirling from out their falling draperies
To melodies that beat a fierce mad call;

No sound of songs that from the hot blood rise,
No langorous, stretching, dusky, velvet maids
Flashing like gleaming weapon their bright eyes,
No swift, wild thrill the quickening blood pervades.

Only mouths widening with a still broad smile
Of comprehension, a strange knowing leer
At white men, at their vanity and guile,
An understanding that fills one with fear.

The beasts in cages much more loyal are,
Restlessly pacing, pacing to and fro,
Dreaming of countries beckoning from afar,
Lands where they roamed in days of long ago.

They burn with an unquenched and smothered fire
Consumed by longings over which they brood,
Oblivious of time, without desire,
Alone and lost in their great solitude.

REMEMBRANCE

Expectant and waiting you muse
On the great rare thing which alone
To enhance your life you would choose:
The awakening of the stone,
The deeps where yourself you would lose.

In the dusk of the shelves, embossed
Shine the volumes in gold and browns,
And you think of countries once crossed,
Of pictures, of shimmering gowns
Of the women that you have lost.

And it comes to you then at last--
And you rise for you are aware
Of a year in the far off past
With its wonder and fear and prayer.

MUSIC

What play you, O Boy? Through the garden it stole
Like wandering steps, like a whisper--then mute;
What play you, O Boy? Lo! your gypsying soul
Is caught and held fast in the pipes of Pan's flute.

And what conjure you? Imprisoned is the song,
It lingers and longs in the reeds where it lies;
Your young life is strong, but how much more strong
Is the longing that through your music sighs.

Let your flute be still and your soul float through
Waves of sound formless as waves of the sea,
For here your song lived and it wisely grew
Before it was forced into melody.

Its wings beat gently, its note no more calls,
Its flight has been spent by you, dreaming Boy!
Now it no longer steals over my walls--
But in my garden I'd woo it to joy.

MAIDEN MELANCHOLY

A young knight comes into my mind
As from some myth of old.

He came! You felt yourself entwined
As a great storm would round you wind.
He went! A blessing undefined
Seemed left, as when church-bells declined
And left you wrapt in prayer.
You fain would cry aloud--but bind
Your scarf about you and tear-blind
Weep softly in its fold.

A young knight comes into my mind
Full armored forth to fare.

His smile was luminously kind
Like glint of ivory enshrined,
Like a home longing undivined,

Like Christmas snows where dark ways wind,
Like sea-pearls about turquoise twined,
Like moonlight silver when combined
With a loved book's rare gold.

MAIDENS AT CONFIRMATION
(Paris in May, 1903)

The white veiled maids to confirmation go
Through deep green garden paths they slowly wind;
Their childhood they are leaving now behind:
The future will be different, they know.

Oh! Will it come? They wait--It must come soon!
The next long hour slowly strikes at last,
The whole house stirs again, the feast is past,
And sadly passes by the afternoon ...

Like resurrection were the garments white
The wreathed procession walked through trees arched wide
Into the church, as cool as silk inside,
With long aisles of tall candles flaming bright:
The lights all shone like jewels rich and rare
To solemn eyes that watched them gleam and flare.

Then through the silence the great song rose high
Up to the vaulted dome like clouds it soared,
Then luminously, gently down it poured--
Over white veils like rain it seemed to die.

The wind through the white garments softly stirred
And they grew vari-coloured in each fold
And each fold hidden blossoms seemed to hold
And flowers and stars and fluting notes of bird,
And dim, quaint figures shimmering like gold
Seemed to come forth from distant myths of old.

Outside the day was one of green and blue,
With touches of a luminous glowing red,
Across the quiet pond the small waves sped.
Beyond the city, gardens hidden from view
Sent odors of sweet blossoms on the breeze
And singing sounded through the far off trees.

It was as though garlands crowned everything
And all things were touched softly by the sun;
And many windows opened one by one
And the light trembled on them glistening.

THE WOMAN WHO LOVES

Ah yes! I long for you. To you I glide
And lose myself--for to you I belong.
The hope that hitherto I have denied
Imperious comes to me as from your side
Serious, unfaltering and swift and strong.

Those times: the times when I was quite alone
By memories wrapt that whispered to me low,
My silence was the quiet of a stone
Over which rippling murmuring waters flow.

But in these weeks of the awakening Spring
Something within me has been freed--something
That in the past dark years unconscious lay,
Which rises now within me and commands
And gives my poor warm life into your hands
Who know not what I was that Yesterday.

PONT DU CARROUSEL

Upon the bridge the blind man stands alone,
Gray like a mist veiled monument he towers
As though of nameless realms the boundary stone
About which circle distant starry hours.

He seems the center around which stars glow
While all earth's ostentations surge below.

Immovably and silently he stands
Placed where the confused current ebbs and flows;
Past fathomless dark depths that he commands
A shallow generation drifting goes....

MADNESS

She thinks: I am--Have you not seen?
Who are you then, Marie?
I am a Queen, I am a Queen!
To your knee, to your knee!

And then she weeps: I was--a child--
Who were you then, Marie?
Know you that I was no man's child,
Poor and in rags--said she.

And then a Princess I became
To whom men bend their knees;
To princes things are not the same
As those a beggar sees.

And those things which have made you great
Came to you, tell me, when?
One night, one night, one night quite late,
Things became different then.

I walked the lane which presently
With strung chords seemed to bend;
Then Marie became Melody
And danced from end to end.

The people watched with startled mien
And passed with frightened glance
For all know that only a Queen
May dance in the lanes: dance!...

LAMENT

Oh! All things are long passed away and far.
A light is shining but the distant star
From which it still comes to me has been dead
A thousand years ... In the dim phantom boat
That glided past some ghastly thing was said.
A clock just struck within some house remote.
Which house?--I long to still my beating heart.
Beneath the sky's vast dome I long to pray ...
Of all the stars there must be far away
A single star which still exists apart.
And I believe that I should know the one
Which has alone endured and which alone
Like a white City that all space commands
At the ray's end in the high heaven stands.

SYMBOLS

From infinite longings finite deeds rise
As fountains spring toward far-off glowing skies,
But rushing swiftly upward weakly bend
And trembling from their lack of power descend--
So through the falling torrent of our fears
Our joyous force leaps like these dancing tears.

NEW POEMS

EARLY APOLLO

As when at times there breaks through branches bare
A morning vibrant with the breath of spring,
About this poet-head a splendour rare
Transforms it almost to a mortal thing.

There is as yet no shadow in his glance,
Too cool his temples for the laurel's glow;
But later o'er those marble brows, perchance,
A rose-garden with bushes tall will grow,

And single petals one by one will fall
O'er the still mouth and break its silent thrall,
--The mouth that trembles with a dawning smile
As though a song were rising there the while.

THE TOMB OF A YOUNG GIRL

We still remember! The same as of yore
All that has happened once again must be.
As grows a lemon-tree upon the shore--
It was like that--your light, small breasts you bore,
And his blood's current coursed like the wild sea.

That god--
who was the wanderer, the slim

Despoiler of fair women; he--the wise,--
But sweet and glowing as your thoughts of him
Who cast a shadow over your young limb
While bending like your arched brows o'er your eyes.

THE POET

You Hour! From me you ever take your flight,
Your swift wings wound me as they whir along;
Without you void would be my day and night,
Without you I'll not capture my great song.

I have no earthly spot where I can live,
I have no love, I have no household fane,
And all the things to which myself I give
Impoverish me with richness they attain.

THE PANTHER

His weary glance, from passing by the bars,
Has grown into a dazed and vacant stare;
It seems to him there are a thousand bars
And out beyond those bars the empty air.

The pad of his strong feet, that ceaseless sound
Of supple tread behind the iron bands,
Is like a dance of strength circling around,
While in the circle, stunned, a great will stands.

But there are times the pupils of his eyes
Dilate, the strong limbs stand alert, apart,
Tense with the flood of visions that arise
Only to sink and die within his heart.

GROWING BLIND

Among all the others there sat a guest
Who sipped her tea as if one apart,
And she held her cup not quite like the rest;
Once she smiled so it pierced one's heart.

When the group of people arose at last
And laughed and talked in a merry tone,
As lingeringly through the rooms they passed
I saw that she followed alone.

Tense and still like one who to sing must rise
Before a throng on a festal night
She lifted her head, and her bright glad eyes
Were like pools which reflected light.

She followed on slowly after the last
As though some object must be passed by,
And yet as if were it once but passed
She would no longer walk but fly.

THE SPANISH DANCER

As a lit match first flickers in the hands
Before it flames, and darts out from all sides
Bright, twitching tongues, so, ringed by growing bands
Of spectators--she, quivering, glowing stands
Poised tensely for the dance--then forward glides

And suddenly becomes a flaming torch.
Her bright hair flames, her burning glances scorch,
And with a daring art at her command
Her whole robe blazes like a fire-brand
From which is stretched each naked arm, awake,
Gleaming and rattling like a frightened snake.

And then, as though the fire fainter grows,
She gathers up the flame--again it glows,
As with proud gesture and imperious air
She flings it to the earth; and it lies there
Furiously flickering and crackling still--
Then haughtily victorious, but with sweet
Swift smile of greeting, she puts forth her will
And stamps the flames out with her small firm feet.

OFFERING

My body glows in every vein and blooms
To fullest flower since I first knew thee,
My walk unconscious pride and power assumes;
Who art thou then--thou who awaitest me?

When from the past I draw myself the while
I lose old traits as leaves of autumn fall;
I only know the radiance of thy smile,
Like the soft gleam of stars, transforming all.

Through childhood's years I wandered unaware
Of shimmering visions my thoughts now arrests
To offer thee, as on an altar fair
That's lighted by the bright flame of thy hair
And wreathed by the blossoms of thy breasts.

LOVE SONG

When my soul touches yours a great chord sings!
How shall I tune it then to other things?
O! That some spot in darkness could be found
That does not vibrate whene'er your depths sound.
But everything that touches you and me
Welds us as played strings sound one melody.
Where is the instrument whence the sounds flow?
And whose the master-hand that holds the bow?
O! Sweet song--

ARCHAIC TORSO OF APOLLO

We cannot fathom his mysterious head,
Through the veiled eyes no flickering ray is sent:
But from his torso gleaming light is shed
As from a candelabrum; inward bent
His glance there glows and lingers. Otherwise
The round breast would not blind you with its grace,
Nor could the soft-curved circle of the thighs
Steal to the arc whence issues a new race.
Nor could this stark and stunted stone display
Vibrance beneath the shoulders heavy bar,
Nor shine like fur upon a beast of prey,
Nor break forth from its lines like a great star--
There is no spot that does not bind you fast
And transport you back, back to a far past.

THE BOOK OF HOURS

The Book of a Monk's Life

I live my life in circles that grow wide
And endlessly unroll,
I may not reach the last, but on I glide
Strong pinioned toward my goal.

About the old tower, dark against the sky,
The beat of my wings hums,
I circle about God, sweep far and high
On through milleniums.

Am I a bird that skims the clouds along,
Or am I a wild storm, or a great song?

Many have painted her. But there was one
Who drew his radiant colours from the sun.
Mysteriously glowing through a background dim
When he was suffering she came to him,
And all the heavy pain within his heart
Rose in his hands and stole into his art.
His canvas is the beautiful bright veil

Through which her sorrow shines. There where the
Texture o'er her sad lips is closely drawn
A trembling smile softly begins to dawn ...
Though angels with seven candles light the place
You cannot read the secret of her face.
In cassocks clad I have had many brothers
In southern cloisters where the laurel grows,
They paint Madonnas like fair human mothers
And I dream of young Titians and of others
In which the God with shining radiance glows.

But though my vigil constantly I keep
My God is dark--like woven texture flowing,
A hundred drinking roots, all intertwined;
I only know that from His warmth I'm growing.
More I know not: my roots lie hidden deep
My branches only are swayed by the wind.

Thou Anxious One! And dost thou then not hear
Against thee all my surging senses sing?
About thy face in circles drawing near
My thought floats like a fluttering white wing.

Dost thou not see, before thee stands my soul
In silence wrapt my Springtime's prayer to pray?
But when thy glance rests on me then my whole
Being quickens and blooms like trees in May.

When thou art dreaming then I am thy Dream,
But when thou art awake I am thy Will
Potent with splendour, radiant and sublime,
Expanding like far space star-lit and still
Into the distant mystic realm of Time.

I love my life's dark hours
In which my senses quicken and grow deep,
While, as from faint incense of faded flowers
Or letters old, I magically steep
Myself in days gone by: again I give
Myself unto the past:--again I live.

Out of my dark hours wisdom dawns apace,
Infinite Life unrolls its boundless space ...

Then I am shaken as a sweeping storm
Shakes a ripe tree that grows above a grave
'Round whose cold clay the roots twine fast and warm--
And Youth's fair visions that glowed bright and brave,
Dreams that were closely cherished and for long,
Are lost once more in sadness and in song.

The Book of Pilgrimage

By day Thou are the Legend and the Dream
That like a whisper floats about all men,
The deep and brooding stillnesses which seem,
After the hour has struck, to close again.

And when the day with drowsy gesture bends
And sinks to sleep beneath the evening skies,
As from each roof a tower of smoke ascends--
So does Thy Realm, my God, around me rise.

All those who seek Thee tempt Thee,
And those who find would bind Thee
To gesture and to form.

But I would comprehend Thee
As the wide Earth unfolds Thee.
Thou growest with my maturity,
Thou Art in calm and storm.

I ask of Thee no vanity
To evidence and prove Thee.
Thou Wert in eons old.

Perform no miracles for me,
But justify Thy laws to me
Which, as the years pass by me.
All soundlessly unfold.

In a house was one who arose from the feast
And went forth to wander in distant lands,
Because there was somewhere far off in the East
A spot which he sought where a great Church stands.
And ever his children, when breaking their bread,
Thought of him and rose up and blessed him as dead.

In another house was the one who had died,
Who still sat at table and drank from the glass
And ever within the walls did abide--
For out of the house he could no more pass.
And his children set forth to seek for the spot
Where stands the great Church which he forgot.

Extinguish my eyes, I still can see you,
Close my ears, I can hear your footsteps fall,
And without feet I still can follow you,
And without voice I still can to you call.
Break off my arms, and I can embrace you,
Enfold you with my heart as with a hand.
Hold my heart, my brain will take fire of you
As flax ignites from a lit fire-brand--
And flame will sweep in a swift rushing flood
Through all the singing currents of my blood.

In the deep nights I dig for you, O Treasure!
To seek you over the wide world I roam,
For all abundance is but meager measure
Of your bright beauty which is yet to come.

Over the road to you the leaves are blowing,
Few follow it, the way is long and steep.
You dwell in solitude--Oh, does your glowing
Heart in some far off valley lie asleep?

My bloody hands, with digging bruised, I've lifted,
Spread like a tree I stretch them in the air
To find you before day to night has drifted;
I reach out into space to seek you there ...

Then, as though with a swift impatient gesture,
Flashing from distant stars on sweeping wing,
You come, and over earth a magic vesture
Steals gently as the rain falls in the spring.

The Book of Poverty and Death

Her mouth is like the mouth of a fine bust
That cannot utter sound, nor breathe, nor kiss,
But that had once from Life received all this
Which shaped its subtle curves, and ever must
From fullness of past knowledge dwell alone,
A thing apart, a parable in stone.

Alone Thou wanderest through space,
Profound One with the hidden face;
Thou art Poverty's great rose,
The eternal metamorphose
Of gold into the light of sun.

Thou art the mystic homeless One;
Into the world Thou never came,
Too mighty Thou, too great to name;
Voice of the storm, Song that the wild wind sings,
Thou Harp that shatters those who play Thy strings!

A watcher of Thy spaces make me,
Make me a listener at Thy stone,
Give to me vision and then wake me
Upon Thy oceans all alone.
Thy rivers' courses let me follow
Where they leap the crags in their flight
And where at dusk in caverns hollow
They croon to music of the night.

Send me far into Thy barren land
Where the snow clouds the wild wind drives,
Where monasteries like gray shrouds stand--
August symbols of unlived lives.
There pilgrims climb slowly one by one,
And behind them a blind man goes:
With him I will walk till day is done
Up the pathway that no one knows ...

Black Eagle Books

www.blackeaglebooks.org
info@blackeaglebooks.org

Black Eagle Books, an independent publisher, was founded as a nonprofit organization in April, 2019. It is our mission to connect and engage the Indian diaspora and the world at large with the best of works of world literature published on a collaborative platform, with special emphasis on foregrounding Contemporary Classics and New Writing.